Published in the UK by
Scamp Publishing
www.scamp-publishing.com

My Baptism Bible ISBN 978-1-83845-349-7
5 Minute Bible Stories ISBN 978-1-83845-348-0

First UK edition 2021
Reprinted 2022, 2024

Publishing Director: Annette Reynolds
Art Director: Gerald Rogers
Pre-production Manager: GingerPromo, Kev Holt

Printed and bound in China

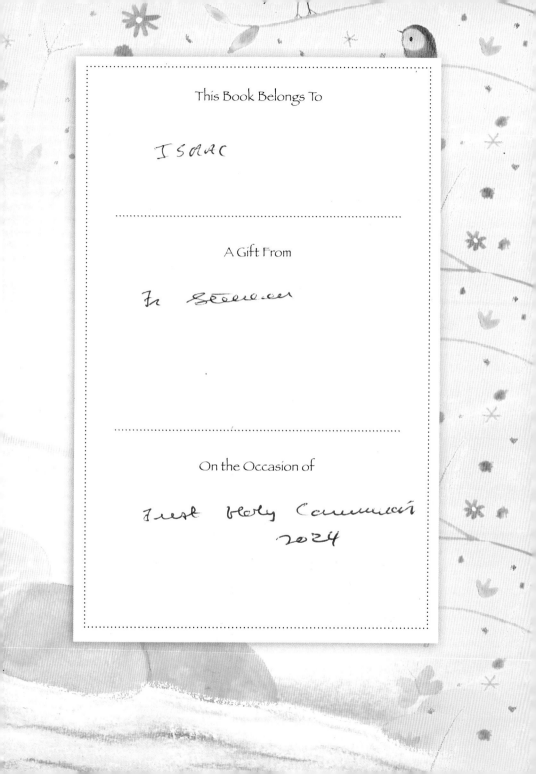

This Book Belongs To

ISAAC

A Gift From

Fr Steele...

On the Occasion of

First Holy Communion
2024

5 MINUTE
BIBLE STORIES

Sally Ann Wright
Illustrated by Dubravka Kolanovic

SCAMP.
PUBLISHING

Contents

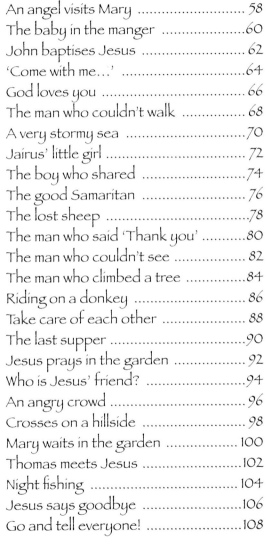

"Children are a blessing and
a gift from the Lord."

Psalm 127:3

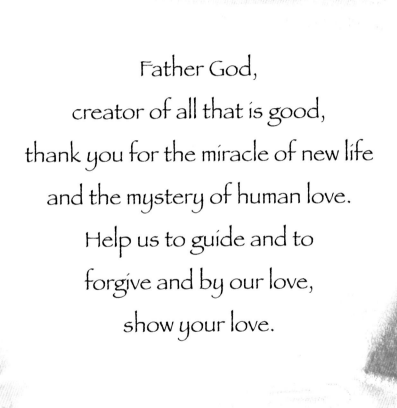

Father God,

creator of all that is good,

thank you for the miracle of new life

and the mystery of human love.

Help us to guide and to

forgive and by our love,

show your love.

The story of creation

Long ago, at the very beginning, God was there.
God made the first light shine in the
darkness. He made high mountains surrounded
by deep water and rushing waterfalls.

God made the leafy trees and bright scented
flowers; the sun, moon and stars.

God made silvery fish and buzzing bees,
song birds and bright butterflies.

God made elephant and hippo,
zebra, rhino and giraffe; cats, dogs, rabbits
and goldfish.

God made people to look after his
beautiful world.

Everything in God's world was good.

A not-so-perfect world

The first people ever were God's friends. Adam and Eve lived in a beautiful garden with a river running through it. God gave them everything they needed to be happy.

'Eat anything you like,' God said, 'except from that tree in the middle of the garden.'

One day a wiggly serpent hissed in Eve's ear. 'Doesn't that fruit look ripe and juicy?' he said.

14

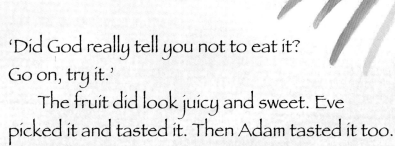

'Did God really tell you not to eat it?
Go on, try it.'

The fruit did look juicy and sweet. Eve
picked it and tasted it. Then Adam tasted it too.

Suddenly everything was different. Adam
and Eve felt ashamed that they had done the
only thing that God had told them not to do.
They felt sad and guilty and they hid from God.

God knew what they had done. God knew
that his world was no longer good and perfect.

Noah's very big boat

'Build an ark,' said God to Noah. 'Save your family and all the animals from the flood that will cover the earth.'

Noah built the ark, a very big boat. All the animals came to Noah, the mummy and the daddy animals, two by two, and Noah kept them safe inside the ark.

And then came the rain – big, loud drops. The puddles turned into a stream and the stream became a river and

the river became a sea of water that covered
everything.

God kept Noah, his family and all the animals
safe inside the ark. When the water went down,
they made their homes on the earth again. And
the mummy and the daddy animals made lots of
babies to make the world beautiful again. And
God sent a beautiful rainbow.

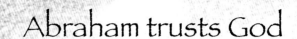

Abraham trusts God

Abraham trusted God. So when God told him to move to a new home in a new country, Abraham took his wife Sarah and his nephew Lot and all

18

his animals. He didn't stop to ask why or how or what would happen next. Abraham just trusted God.

They didn't know where they were going and they didn't know how long it would take them.

Abraham and Sarah had no children but, one starry night, God made them a promise.

'Come and look at the stars,' God said. 'Can you count them? No! But one day there will be as many people in your family as there are stars in the sky.'

Abraham still trusted God. He waited a long time but Abraham and Sarah were very happy when baby Isaac was born. It was the start of their very big family.

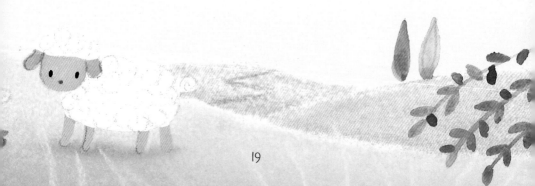

Abraham is a grandpa

When Isaac was a man, Abraham wanted him to marry a girl who loved God too. He was very happy when Isaac married Rebekah.

They were all very happy when Rebekah gave birth to twins – two little baby boys and twice as much work!

The boys were very different. Esau had lots of red hair. Jacob didn't have much hair at all.

They grew up to be different too. Esau became a hunter, an outdoor man. His father loved him best of all. Jacob loved to cook. He was good company for his mother and she loved him best of all.

A very special blessing

Isaac couldn't walk far any more. He wasn't very strong and he could no longer see very well at all. Isaac knew he was getting to be a very old man and he wanted to bless his first son before he died.

One day he asked Esau to go hunting. 'Come back and cook me my favourite meal and then I will ask God to bless you,' he said.

But while Esau was gone, Rebekah

helped Jacob dress up in Esau's smelly clothes
and put hairy animal skins on his arms and neck.
Then she cooked a lovely meal for Isaac.

'You smell like Esau and you feel like Esau,'
said Isaac. 'But you sound like Jacob. Are you
sure you are my first son?' said Isaac. But when
Jacob said yes, his father blessed him. 'May God
bless you always and give you good things all the
days of your life...'

Jacob had stolen Esau's
special blessing – and
Esau was very angry
when he found out!

23

Joseph's special coat

God did bless Jacob. He left home and fell in love
with Rachel. After a while he had children, many
children – twelve sons and a daughter! But like his
parents before him, Jacob had a favourite son.

    Joseph was that son, Rachael's first child.
Joseph knew that his father loved him more than
his brothers and sometimes it made him proud and
boastful. So when Jacob gave him a beautiful coat,
his brothers were very unhappy – so unhappy
that they began to plot to get rid of him.

They waited for the right moment – and sold him as a slave to some passing traders on their way to Egypt.

The brothers told Jacob that his favourite son had been killed by a wild animal. Jacob was sure he would never be happy again.

The king's bad dreams

Joseph was alone, in a strange land, away from his family, away from the father who loved him. And Joseph was a slave. But God looked after him all the time he was in Egypt.

Joseph worked hard for his master and was almost happy until… his master's wife told lies about him. Joseph was sent to prison. But while he was there, he met a man who knew the great king of Egypt.

The man told the king that God helped Joseph to understand dreams – and the king asked Joseph to help him.

'I have had some strange dreams,' the king told Joseph. 'Help me to understand my dreams so I can sleep again!'

Good things come
from bad

Joseph did help the king. God was warning the king that soon there would be a terrible time when everyone would be hungry. But first there would be plenty of good harvests.

'You must store up all the grain from the good harvests so there will be enough for everyone to share when the bad times come,' said Joseph. 'You need someone to help you make this happen.'

The king smiled. 'You shall be that man!' he said.

Joseph became so important that he invited all his family and all their families to live with him in Egypt where there was enough food to eat. God was taking care of them all.

Jacob was very happy to know that his dead son was alive after all... and Joseph forgave his brothers for what they had done to him.

So it was that Abraham's VERY big family made their home in Egypt for many, many years.

29

A baby in a basket

Joseph died when he was an old man, but his family grew and grew until you couldn't count how many of them there were.

There was a new king in Egypt, a bad king who was afraid of all the people who lived in his land but who were strangers to him. The bad king made them work hard as his slaves. Then he sent his soldiers to

throw all their baby boys into the River Nile!

Miriam watched her mother hide her baby brother in a basket by the river.

After a while, a princess found the basket. 'You must belong to one of the slaves,' she said. 'I will keep you. You will be called Moses.'

God was taking caring of Moses. Big sister Miriam brought her mother to the princess so she could be his nurse.

Frogs, flies and buzzy things

Moses grew up in the king's palace but he saw that his family and friends were badly treated; he hated it. Then one day he saw one of them being beaten by an Egyptian. Moses was so angry, he killed the man. He was so afraid the king would find out that he ran away.

Moses made his home in the desert. Then one day God spoke to him from a burning bush. It was time to go back to see the king.

'Tell him to let my people go!' said God.

Moses went to the king – but the king did not want to! The king didn't know God – and these people were his slaves!

So ten terrible plagues were seen in Egypt with frogs and flies and all sorts of horrible things invading the land until… the king told Moses to take the people and GO!

The road to freedom

God appeared as a tall cloud to show them the way to go every day; God appeared as a tall fire to show them the way to go every night.

When they reached the Red Sea, Moses lifted his stick and the wind blew a path across the sea so everyone could cross over safely on dry land.

God's people were no longer slaves in Egypt! They were free!

God provided food when the people were hungry. God provided water when they were thirsty.

The ten commandments

God gave Moses rules to help them live together so they could be happy with each other and live in peace. The best of these rules are called the ten commandments. Some of them are about things we should do and others about things we shouldn't do.

'I am your God, the true and living God who made heaven and earth. Do not worship any other.

'Don't make anything else into a god and worship it.

'The name of God is special and holy. Use it when you pray, but do not use it as a swear word.

'Keep one day special so you can rest and have time to worship together.

'Life is precious. Don't murder anyone.

'Don't steal someone else's husband or wife.

'Don't steal anything!

'Don't tell lies about other people.

'Don't be jealous of things other people have.'

The rules were written on two great pieces of stone which God's people took care of and carried them wherever they went.

Gideon trusts God

Gideon was hiding. He was, like all his friends, afraid of the fierce Midianites who lived close by. They would attack on camels and steal all their food. Gideon and his friends were afraid and they were hungry.

But then an angel visited Gideon. 'God has chosen you to help his people,' said the angel.

'But I am not brave or clever,' said Gideon. 'Why would God want me?'

Gideon needed God to show him a sign – so he could be completely sure God had chosen him.

Gideon put out a woolly fleece one night and asked God to make it wet when the ground was dry. And God did. Then Gideon asked God to make the woolly fleece dry when the ground was wet with dew. And God did!

Gideon trusted God to help him. Gideon made the Midianites go away so he and all his friends were no longer afraid and could live in peace.

David and Goliath

David was a shepherd boy. He had seven big
brothers, and the three biggest were in the king's
army. So when David went to see them, he also
saw Goliath.

David watched the big scary giant march up
and down shouting with his big scary voice, 'Who
will come and fight me?'

Goliath wore big scary armour and had a big
scary sword. He frightened the soldiers – he
even frightened King Saul!

'Who does he think he is?' said David. 'God
is much greater than a giant! I will fight him. God

has always helped me fight lions and bears when I looked after my father's sheep. I know he will help me now.'

The King offered David his own armour but it was TOO big. The king offered David his sword but it was TOO heavy. Instead David whirled a pebble around in his sling. Then... crash! Goliath fell to the ground with a big scary noise! Now he wouldn't frighten anyone again!

God's gift to Solomon

Solomon was a very young man when he became king.

'What gift would you like me to give you?' God asked him.

Did Solomon want to have lots of money? Did he want to be famous? Did he want to live for ever?

'I would like to be a good man and make the right choices. I want to be fair and do the right things,' said Solomon. 'I want to be a good king who rules his people well.'

God was so pleased with Solomon's answer that he gave Solomon all he asked for and even more — he made him good and wise, fair and just — but he also made him rich and famous and gave him a long life.

People everywhere knew that God had blessed Solomon.

A very wise king

King Solomon looked at the two women in front
of him.

'This is my baby,' said one woman. 'This woman
and I live in the same house. I gave birth to this
baby boy, and two days later she had a baby boy
too. But her baby died – so while I was sleeping,
she took my baby and put her dead baby next to
me. Now she is telling everyone my child is hers.'

'No!' said the other woman. 'The living child is
mine! Hers is the child who died.'

Then the two women began to argue over the
baby boy.

Solomon called for a sword.

'Cut the living baby in two pieces,' said the
king. 'Give each woman half of the child.'

The first woman screamed, 'No! Don't hurt my
baby. Give her the child.'

The other woman said, 'Yes, that's fair.
Cut the baby in two pieces.'

'Stop!' said wise King Solomon. 'This is the

child's mother. Give him to her.'

Solomon knew that the real mother would rather give her baby away than let anyone hurt him.

When people heard what had happened, they knew that God had made the king wise and good.

God takes care of Elijah

It had stopped raining. The earth was hot and dry and thirsty. The people were hot and dry and thirsty.

King Ahab had stopped talking to the living God. He didn't believe God was the one who

gave them rain and made the plants grow to give them food. So God stopped sending the rain.

But Elijah loved and trusted God. Elijah was God's friend. God told Elijah where he could find a little stream with cool, clear water. God sent large black ravens to Elijah with food in their beaks. God took care of Elijah.

Just enough to share

When the stream dried up, and there was no water left, God told Elijah where he should go next.

'Go to Zarephath,' said God. 'You will find a woman there who will help you.'

When Elijah arrived at the village he was hot and tired and dusty. But he found a woman gathering sticks to make a fire.

'Will you give me some water – and perhaps some bread to eat?' Elijah asked.

The woman looked sadly at Elijah. 'I have none to give you, Sir,' she replied. 'I am making my last piece of bread to share with my son – then we shall starve, for there will be no flour left in the jar and not one drop of oil.'

'Please share your last meal with me,' said Elijah. 'God will make sure you do not go hungry.'

Elijah watched as the woman baked the bread and then he shared the meal with her and her son.

When the woman went back she found that there was just enough flour to make more bread and just enough oil… and there was just enough each time she baked so that she could share another meal with Elijah and her son and always have enough for more.

God looked after them all.

Fire and rain

King Ahab worshipped a stone statue. After three years with no rain, did he still believe that this statue made the rain fall from the sky?

The king and all those who worshipped the statue met with Elijah on Mount Carmel.

'Our God is the living God,' said Elijah. 'Surely you know that? So why are you worshipping a stone statue? We will ask our Gods to send down fire. Then you can choose who to worship.'

The people called on the stone statue to light the fire. They danced and they shouted and they asked again – but nothing happened.

Then Elijah spoke to God. Everyone watched. 'Lord, let everyone here see and know that you alone are the one true and living God,' he prayed.

And fire fell from heaven. The people were amazed! Then they knew that God was the living God and they worshipped him.

Then God sent rain once more to water the earth.

Jonah and the big fish

The people who lived in Nineveh were cruel and wicked. Jonah knew that and thought they deserved God's punishment. So when God asked him to go and take them a message, he didn't want to go. Instead, he ran away!

Jonah got on a ship going in the opposite direction. He forgot that you can't run away from God.

The wind howled and the waves crashed and

the ship was tossed up and down. Jonah knew it
was all his fault.

'Throw me into the sea!' said Jonah. 'I am
running away from God – but you don't need to
be harmed.'

The sailors threw him overboard... and Jonah
called on God to help him. A huge sea creature
came to catch Jonah and swallowed him whole.

The God who forgives

Jonah sat inside the fish and prayed…
   'Lord, I was wrong. You are a great and
wonderful God and when I called, you helped me.
I am sorry I ran away. I should have listened.
I should have done as you asked. I will do it now
– send me to Nineveh.'
   The big fish spat Jonah out of its mouth
on to dry land and Jonah took God's message
to Nineveh.

When the people heard that God was angry with them for being cruel and wicked, they didn't laugh at Jonah or at God. Instead they listened. They listened and they said sorry – and they showed they were sorry. Even the king was sorry. They asked God to forgive them and help them change their ways.

So God, who is kind and caring, and loves it when people stop doing bad things, forgave the wicked people of Nineveh (even though it made Jonah grumpy!).

Daniel and the lions

Daniel was the king of Babylon's friend.
Daniel was also God's friend. Daniel
loved God and prayed to him three
times every day.

But the kings' men were not Daniel's
friends. They didn't like Daniel at all.

'Let's make a new law,' they told the king.
'People must pray to YOU and only you,
because you are great and powerful – but if they
don't… they should be thrown to the lions.'

Daniel heard about the new law but he still
loved God; so he prayed to him three times
every day, just as he had before. The king had
no choice. He had to have Daniel thrown to the
lions. The king was very sad – but the kings' men
were very happy!

When the king went to the lions' den the next
morning, he was surprised – and very happy – to

find Daniel still alive and well!

'Here I am!' said Daniel. 'My God is able to keep me safe – even from these lions.'

'Your God really IS great and powerful,' said the king. And then he made a new law: 'Everyone should worship Daniel's God from now on because he is a great God.'

An angel visits Mary

Mary was just an ordinary girl when God chose her to do something very special. One day he sent the angel Gabriel to see her.

'Don't be afraid,' said the angel. 'God has sent me to tell you that you are going to have a baby. The baby will be God's own Son and Jesus will be his name.'

'But I don't have a husband yet,' said Mary. 'How can I have a baby?'

'Nothing is impossible for God,' said the angel. 'Trust him.'

Mary was a little afraid, but she was also happy. She told Joseph about the angel's message and he promised to take care of her and God's Son. Not long afterwards, Mary found she was expecting a baby.

The baby in the manger

Joseph took Mary to Bethlehem, because he was descended from King David. The Roman Emperor wanted everyone to return to the home of their families so he could count his people.

While they were there, Mary gave birth to her baby son. She made a bed for Jesus in the manger, because there was no room for them at the inn.

That night, angels appeared in the sky, bringing the good news of Jesus' birth to some shepherds who were looking after their sheep.

The shepherds went to look for the baby, the one whom God had sent to save all the people on earth. They found him with Mary and Joseph and told them about the message of the angels.

John baptises Jesus

Jesus was a good little boy who grew up to be a good man.

One day he went to see John, who was baptising people in the River Jordan.

'Come and tell God you are sorry for the

bad things you have done,' said John to anyone who would listen. 'Tell him you want to do good things. Show him you are sorry by coming to be baptised.'

'Baptise me,' said Jesus. John knew immediately who Jesus was.

'But you don't need to be baptised,' said John. 'You have done no bad things!'

'Please, I want to do this,' said Jesus.

So John baptised him.

Then they heard God's voice from heaven, 'This is my son. I love him.'

'Come with me…'

Jesus grew up in Capernaum on the banks of Lake Galilee. He knew many of the fishermen there.

'Come with me,' Jesus said to Peter and Andrew.'

'Come with me,' he said to James and John.

'Leave your fishing nets and help me tell people how good God is. Help me to make bad people good and sad people happy. Help me heal people who are blind or deaf or cannot walk.'

'Come with me,' Jesus called to Matthew, the

man who collected taxes for the Romans.

Twelve men left what they were doing and decided to be disciples, special friends of Jesus who went wherever he was and learned more about what God wanted of everyone. They were brothers Peter and Andrew, brothers James and John, Philip, Bartholomew, Matthew, Thomas, another James, Thaddeus, Simon and Judas.

God loves you

'God loves you and cares about you,' Jesus told everyone. 'Don't worry too much about your next meal or what you are going to wear. Be like the birds in the sky – God provides food for them and they don't go hungry. Be like the flowers in the fields – God makes every one of them beautiful!

'Trust God – he will give you what you need. Love God – and share what you have with each other.'

'God cares what happens to the tiniest sparrow, and you are much more important to God than the sparrow. God knows you and he cares about you. God will keep you safe in his strong, kind hands. Trust God.'

The man who couldn't walk

'Excuse me!'

'Be careful now!'

Lifting their friend carefully through all the people and then up the steps beside the house was not easy. But the four men wanted their friend to meet Jesus. They wanted Jesus to meet their friend – and help him to walk again!

The crowd was a problem. So they planned to make a hole in the roof and lower him down into the room below where Jesus was talking to a crowd of people.

The plan worked.

Jesus knew just what they wanted. And

Jesus healed their friend so that he could pick himself up and walk home! People could hardly believe what had happened in that room that day. Who was Jesus? How did he do that?

A very stormy sea

Jesus sailed in a fishing boat across Lake Galilee
with his friends. It had been a very busy day
and soon Jesus fell asleep to the sound of the
gentle waves.

The storm came suddenly, with a howling
wind and loud claps of thunder; with whooshing
waves that rocked the boat up and down, up
and down…

'Wake up!' the men shouted to the sleeping
Jesus. 'Help us! We are all going to drown!'

Jesus stood up and told the wind to drop.

Jesus spoke to the waves and told them to stop. And just as suddenly as it had started, everything was calm again.

Jesus' friends looked at Jesus in amazement. How could a man have stopped a raging storm?

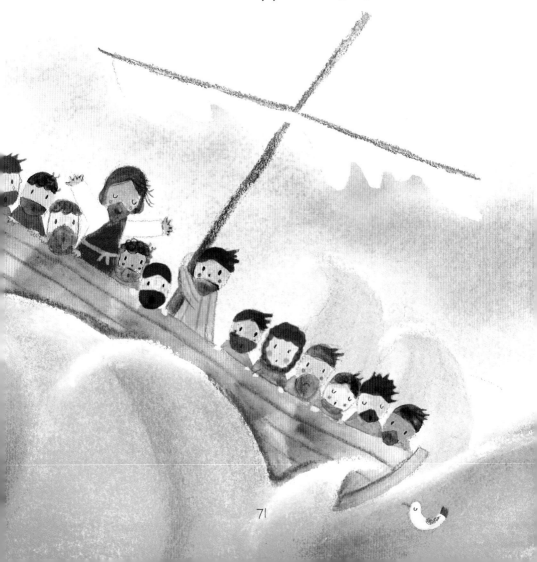

Jairus' little girl

'Please come and help my daughter!' Jairus was almost pulling Jesus through the crowd of people. 'She is very ill…'

Jesus went with Jairus. But there were many people there who also wanted Jesus to help them and before they reached the house, a man came to tell Jairus that it was too late.

'I'm so sorry – but your little girl has died.'

'Trust me,' Jesus said to Jairus, gently.

They went into Jairus' house and Jesus took his daughter's hand in his.

'Wake up, little girl,' Jesus said.

Jairus' daughter opened her eyes and smiled at Jesus.

'I think she would like something to eat,' said Jesus, smiling at her happy parents.

73

The boy who shared

There were thousands of hungry people out on the hillside.

They had been listening all day to Jesus tell stories about how much God loved them. They had seen Jesus healing people who were blind or deaf or hurting. But now it was late.

'You can share my lunch,' a little boy offered. There were five pieces of bread and two little fish.

'Thank you,' smiled Jesus. Then he thanked God too.

The disciples shared out the picnic with all the many people there – each one sharing with the one next to him or her… and somehow no one went away hungry. There were even twelve baskets of leftovers – all from that little boy's lunch. God had blessed them all.

The good Samaritan

'God wants you to be kind to other people –
even if you don't know them,' said Jesus.

   'Once a man was attacked and robbed while
walking on a lonely road. The man hurt so much
he thought he would die.

   'After a while, he heard someone coming.
Surely this man would help him? But instead the
man walked past him down the road.

'Later he heard someone else coming. If only this man would stop… but he carried on walking without stopping too.

'Then the man heard the sound of a donkey clip-clopping along the road. Its owner was a Samaritan. Surely he wouldn't help a stranger…? But he stopped, bathed the man's wounds, helped him on to his donkey and took him to an inn. He paid for the innkeeper to take care of him till he was well.

'Be kind to people whoever they are,' said Jesus, 'just like the Good Samaritan. Treat others the way you want them to treat you.'

The lost sheep

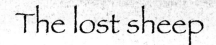

'God is like a good shepherd,' said Jesus. 'He knows his sheep by name and every one of them is important to him.'

'Imagine you have a hundred sheep. One day you find that there are only ninety-nine – one has wandered off by itself, lost and frightened. Do you feel happy that you still have ninety-nine sheep safe in the fold? No! You climb hills and look in prickly bushes and you don't rest until you hear the faint cry of that one lost sheep.

'Then you carry it home on your shoulders, so happy that your lost sheep is found that you invite your friends to celebrate with you!

'That's how God feels about just one of his children who forgets that God loves him and feels lost and alone.'

The man who said 'Thank you'

As Jesus approached a village one day he saw ten men standing in a huddle. They were hiding their faces, afraid to come near, frightened to be seen. But they knew Jesus might be able to help them.

Jesus knew they suffered from leprosy, a bad skin disease that made their lives miserable.

'Go back to your homes,' said Jesus. 'Don't be afraid – God has healed you.'

It was a miracle! Nine of the men hurried home, but one man came to speak to Jesus.

'Thank you!' the man said. 'Thank you so much for healing me.'

Jesus smiled kindly at the man. But he looked sadly at the others in the distance, wondering why no one else had said thank you...

The man who couldn't see

What was all that noise? It was a crowd, a huge crowd of people – and they were following Jesus!

Bartimaeus put down his begging bowl. He knew that name! Jesus had healed people who couldn't hear and walk and …

'Jesus!' he shouted. 'I'm over here!'

People tried to ssshhh him. But the blind man knew who Jesus was. He knew that Jesus could heal him too.

'JESUS!' he shouted, even more loudly. 'I'm over here!'

Jesus stopped to listen. 'What can I do for you?' he asked.

'Please – I just want to see!' the man said.

Jesus healed him. The first thing Bartimaeus saw when his eyes were opened was the kind smiling face of Jesus. Then Bartimaeus joined the crowd of people following Jesus along the road.

The man who climbed a tree

Zacchaeus was a bit too old to be climbing trees. But Jesus was here in Jericho – and he wanted so much to see him.

The road was lined with crowds of people walking with Jesus, eager to see the man who was a friend to everyone, the man who made people well, the man who said God loved them…

Zacchaeus needed a friend. No one liked him because he worked for the Romans – and because he had cheated lots of people out of their money. Three coins for the Romans and one for Zacchaeus…

But now Jesus was looking right at him.

'Come down,' said Jesus. 'I'd like to come to your house today.'

Zacchaeus couldn't get down the tree fast enough! Not long afterwards, Zacchaeus knew

that Jesus was his friend – and he started to share his money with the poor and repay the people he had cheated.

'That's why I'm here,' said Jesus, 'to help people like Zacchaeus.'

Riding on a donkey

Crowds of people were making their way into Jerusalem. Jesus and his friends were among them, all going for the Passover Festival.

Jesus was riding on a young donkey, trotting slowly through the gates of the city.

'Look! Here comes Jesus!' someone shouted. 'Hooray for Jesus! Jesus is our king!'

People started to wave and cheer. Others waved palm branches. Lots of them knew about the good things Jesus had done. They knew someone he had helped or healed – someone who could now walk, or hear or see… Many had heard the stories he told. They loved him.

But not everyone was happy. Some of the holy men stood to one side, frowning and plotting.

Take care of each other

Later in the week, Jesus and his friends met in an upstairs room to eat together. But before they sat down, Jesus knelt and washed the dust from their feet and dried them gently with a towel.

Peter was shocked. Surely this was a servant's job!

'You must let me do this, Peter, if you are my friend,' said Jesus. 'If I can do this for you, perhaps you will also do it for each other. No one is too important to look after someone else. This is how people know that you are my friends. Take care of each other. Love one another in this way.'

The last supper

Jesus gave some food to Judas. He knew that the man who had once been his friend had taken thirty silver coins to betray him to the religious leaders.

'Not all of you here are my friends,' Jesus said, looking at Judas.

'I would do anything for you, Lord,' Peter said. 'I would even die for you!' The others said the same.

'Peter, before the cock crows in the morning you will say three times that you don't even know me,' said Jesus sadly. Peter shook his head, confused.

Jesus shared the bread with them. 'This is my body broken for you,' he said. He shared a cup of wine. 'This is my blood, spilled for you.'

The men looked at each other. What did Jesus mean?

Jesus prays in the garden

After supper, Jesus took his friends to a garden full of olive trees. They looked silver in the moonlight.

'Keep watch while I pray,' said Jesus. He looked very sad.

'I will do anything you ask of me, Father God,' said Jesus. 'But please, help me to be brave.'

When Jesus went back to his friends, he

found they had fallen asleep while he was
praying. Jesus felt very lonely. They woke to
hear the sounds of people coming through the
darkness, their torches shining on their swords.

Judas came forward to greet Jesus with a
kiss. It was a sign. The soldiers arrested Jesus
and marched him away while his friends
ran away.

Who is Jesus' friend?

Peter and John stayed close by, hiding in the darkness. They followed at a safe distance to see what was happening to Jesus.

Peter was afraid. He stood in the courtyard lit by the firelight. He watched and listened.

'I know you,' said a servant. 'You were with that man in there.'

'No,' said Peter. 'That wasn't me.'

'You're right,' said another. 'You're one of his friends.'

'I'm not!' said Peter.

'Yes, you are!' said another. 'You have the same northern accent.'

'No, you're wrong. Jesus is not my friend!' Peter said.

At that moment Jesus

was led out from the room where he was being questioned. He looked at Peter sadly. And Peter remembered what he had promised at supper – and he hid his face and cried.

An angry crowd

The holy men who had been asking Jesus questions all night knew that he had done nothing wrong. But they wanted him out of the way. They took him to Pontius Pilate because only the Roman governor could ask for his death...

Pilate knew that Jesus was innocent too. But he didn't want to make the holy men angry.

'Who should I release today for Passover?' Pilate asked the crowd. 'Jesus – the man you call your king? Or Barabbas, the murderer in the dungeon?'

There were people in the crowd who had been bribed. 'We want Barabbas!' they shouted.

Pilate had not expected that. 'Then what shall I do with Jesus?' he asked.

'Crucify him!' they shouted. 'Crucify him!'

Pilate washed his hands in a basin of water. 'Take him away,' he told the soldiers.

Crosses on a hillside

They put a crown made out of sharp thorns on his head.

'Here you are, King Jesus!' they laughed. 'How do you like your crown?'

He was made to carry a heavy cross up the hill. The people in the crowds stared at him. Some cried as he stumbled. They could not believe what was happening.

Jesus, the man who had healed people, helped them and been kind to them, was crucified on the hillside between two thieves.

'Forgive them, Father,' Jesus prayed from the cross. 'They don't know what they are doing.'

Jesus was dying for the soldiers and for everyone in the world so that God would forgive them for everything they'd ever done wrong.

Many painful hours later, Jesus took his last breath and died.

Mary waits in the garden

One of Jesus' friends offered to take Jesus from the cross and bury him before sunset that Friday evening. A big, heavy stone door was rolled in front of the rock cave to shut it tight.

Early on Sunday morning, some of the women who had been his friends went to the garden where the burial place was. They saw that the big, heavy stone door had been rolled away – and the cave was empty!

'Jesus isn't here,' said an angel. 'God has brought him back from the place of the dead – he is alive again!'

Some of the women ran from the garden to tell the others, but Mary Magdalene stayed by

the empty cave, crying. Then she heard a kind voice behind her.

'Mary,' he said.

Mary heard the voice of Jesus! Jesus was alive and Mary had seen him!

Thomas meets Jesus

Later Jesus went to see his other friends. Some of them were together behind locked doors, still afraid. But suddenly Jesus was there with them in the room! They were so pleased they could hardly believe it. Here was Jesus – and he was alive!

Jesus stayed and shared a meal with them. But Thomas had not been there.

'I can't believe it,' said Thomas. 'I won't believe Jesus is alive unless I see him myself.'

'But it's true,' said his friends. 'We've seen him. We've spoken to him.'

A week later, Jesus came again. This time Thomas was there.

'Hello, Thomas,' said Jesus. 'Look at me. Touch the wounds in my hands. Now do you

believe that it's me – and I'm alive?'

    'Jesus!' gasped Thomas. 'It really is you!'
And Thomas fell to his knees. 'You are my Lord
and my God.'

Night fishing

Peter and his friends hadn't seen Jesus for a few days.

'I'm going fishing,' said Peter one night.

Six of his friends went too. They fished all night, but they didn't catch any fish at all, not one. At sunrise, they heard a man's voice from the shore.

'Have you caught anything?' he called.

'Nothing,' they shouted back.

'Put out your net on the other side,'
said the man.

They tried once more – and suddenly the net
was full to bursting with slippery, silvery fish!

'It's Jesus!' Peter said, jumping into the water.

The friends joined Jesus for breakfast on
the beach, with some of the fish and warm bread.
And while they talked, Peter knew that Jesus
had forgiven him for saying he was not his friend.
They were friends once more.

Jesus says goodbye

Jesus stayed with his friends for a while. They loved hearing him talk again. They listened even more carefully.

'Go and tell everyone everywhere what you have learned from me. Help them to know and love God, baptise them, and teach them to love others too.'

Jesus told them to wait in Jerusalem for the Holy Spirit to come to help them. Then it would be as if he were there with all of them all the time. They would never be alone.

Then Jesus left them to go to his father in heaven. The disciples were happy, knowing that Jesus was preparing a home for them and would come back again for them one day.

Go and tell everyone!

God sent the Holy Spirit to help Peter and John and his other friends. The Spirit came as a rushing wind and as fire. They weren't frightened any more. They were bold and brave!

'Jesus is God's Son,' Peter said to huge crowds of people. 'He died on a cross because he loves you. Stop doing bad things. Tell Jesus you are sorry and he will forgive you.'

Thousands of people heard what Peter said. Thousands believed and decided to trust God after listening to Peter. They prayed and had meals together. They shared what they owned and took care of each other – just as Jesus had taught them. Their lives were changed completely. And they knew that God was always there to help them.